INTRODUCTION

Dr. John S. Smith, MA, PhD, FSAScot. Senior lecturer in the Department of Geography, University of Aberdeen. An expert in local history, he is editor of the Local Studies series of the University's Centre for Scottish Studies. He is author of many books and articles on historical geography including 'George Washinton Wilson's Aberdeen' and the volume 'Caithness and Sutherland' in the Third Statistical Account.

The late Victorian photographs which form the baseline for our glimpse into "the sparkling cage" recall a time when life was leisurely, when Aberdeen combined a spirit of considerable entrepreneurial flair with a measure of urban squalor. The commercial photographers of the period tended to focus on the former rather than the latter. Although the contemporary photographs reveal significant changes, yet the granite from Rubislaw's great hole – from whence, it was claimed, half of Aberdeen came – has provided a lasting memorial to the Victorian economic miracle, to the skills of local masons and architects, and a fitting reminder of the enduring durability of our native rock. Many of the contemporary views are eloquent of the often frantic pace of life tolerated by modern urbanites, whether on foot or on wheels. The photographic fodder for **The Sparkling Cage** has been provided by courtesy of the University of Aberdeen, from the surviving glass plate negatives of George Washington Wilson and Company, an Aberdeen firm which pioneered the techniques, and the product marketing, of landscape photography. The prints of Aberdeen and Deeside were originally sold through a local bookshop, run by Wilson's friend, George Walker. Wilson's original reputation, based on a photographic contract with the Royal Family at Balmoral, expanded to capture the street scenes and port activities of Aberdeen as well as most other Scottish cities, towns and villages. The quality of the product established George Washington Wilson as a photographer of international repute. A succession of printing premise locations in Aberdeen culminated in a large works in St. Swithins Street, with a new house at Queen's Cross – now **The Albyn** – and continued expansion of the company, with the registered trade mark GWW. The team of photographers employed by the company stuck closely to Wilson's high standards and style. The company, eventually run by Wilson's three sons, John Hay, Louis and Charles, continued to expand its range of stock both within the United Kingdom and beyond, but, in the face of major rivals like Valentines of Dundee, was eventually declared bankrupt in 1908. In 1954, the surviving 40,000 glass plate negatives were donated to Aberdeen University Library by the Aberdeen photographer, the late Archie Strachan. The collection forms a unique social document for the period. The selection of GWW photographs presented here concentrates on the major elements and arteries of Aberdeen's townscape, and includes many photographs not previously published. These should be of interest to resident and visitor alike. The contemporary views help us to focus on the unique character of our Granite City, still surviving relatively intact, despite the efforts of successive sets of innovative councillors.

John S. Smith

Aberdeen

Mica glittered from the white stone.
Town of the pure crystal,
I learnt Latin in your sparkling cage,
I loved your brilliant streets.

Places that have been good to us we love.
The rest we are resigned to.
The fishermen hung shining in their yellow
among university bells.

Green lawns and clinging ivy. Mediaeval
your comfortable lectures, your calm grammar.
The plate glass windows showed their necklaces
like writhing North Sea fish.

Nothing will die, even the lies we learn!
Union street was an arrow
debouching on the crooked lanes, where women
sweated like leaking walls.

Iain Crichton Smith

The sparkling Kemnay granite 'cage' of Marischal College.

Aberdeen's early 16th century Bridge of Dee pictured at a time when it lay virtually in open countryside. Despite widening and strengthening, it retains its original exterior form, and bears many coats of arms, mostly those of Bishop Gavin Dunbar.

Only the haughlands of the Dee remain as open space. Offices and council blocks remain surprisingly subordinate to church spires in the urban skyscape.

The baronial elegance of the New Town House (1868-74) – in which some observers detect a Flemish influence – is flanked by the Old Tolbooth, partly revamped, but basically of the 17th century. The feeling of street spaciousness results from the absence of trams and buses.

3

Pedestrianised Castle Street is here sadly devoid of people, as well as traffic. The elegant simplicity of the buildings beyond the New Town House, originally conceived as residences, is no longer in evidence. The Athenaeum has risen from the ashes of 1973.

Aberdeen's Mercat Cross, arguably the finest in Scotland, dates from the 17th century, although restored by John Smith in 1820. The Georgian building in the right background, demolished to permit the widening of Justice Street in the 1890's, was the Record Office.

Seaton brick gables contrast with the granite fronted houses on the north side of the Castlegate.

Castle Street – formerly the heart of historical Aberdeen – photographed on a flagday? The boarded up buildings conceal a declared City District intent to restore the Castlegate to its rightful social and architectural position in city life.

Brian Kiloh

Brian Kiloh

6

Ceres rules OK on the corner porch of the Clydesdale Bank with the Duke of Gordon, Aberdeen's first polished granite statue (1844) keeping a watchful eye on events. The Duke now resides in Golden Square.

Although never quite achieving the original architectural unity of Union Street, King Street promised much in its lower section. Castle Street, now pedestrianised on an experimental basis, bids fair to becoming something of a daytime meeting place again, a role which it fulfilled during much of the 19th century.

Aberdeen's Friday, Castle Street Market is apparently presided over by the Duke of Gordon (in Castle Street 1842-1952). The eventual construction of a tramway loop ended this obviously popular market.

A successor trader's market in Castle Street was re-introduced in 1988. However the heyday of open-air, and closed markets, was in the prewar days before the emergence of chain stores, supermarkets and shopping centres.

The Mannie is now rightfully restored to plainstanes where Aberdonians await buses rather than discuss business matters.

10

CASTLE ST. & MUNICIPAL BUILDINGS, ABERDEEN. 5314. G.W.W.

A Russian cannon captured at the seige of Sevastopol during the Crimean War and presented to Aberdeen by the War Office is on display. A coachman awaits his fare at a time when this part of the town retained a substantial residential presence.

Pedalling in the pedestrianised precinct of the Castlegate.

Brian Kiloh

A topless tram en route the Sea Beach outside Union Chambers, designed for visitors anxious to partake of the sea air. For the Queen's Cross run, the trams were sedately open-fronted.

AUL F796

13

In this early 20th century view of Union Street, trams progress at a leisurely pace, including No. 8 to suburban Bieldside. Shop signs pronounce the presence of specialist milliners and hatters, and their products are much in evidence amongst passers-by.

This is the age of the bus and car, and street building uses change relatively frequently.

St. Nicholas Street in its heyday as a shopping street with open-topped horse trams conveying passengers to Kittybrewster. The statue of Queen Victoria (version two – in bronze) is now sited at Queen's Cross.

Brian Kiloh

In 1989, pedestrians are making a come-back with the St. Nicholas Centre sited adjacent to Marks and Spencers and Carnegie's Brae roofed for shoppers queuing at Europe's busiest speed bank.

The Wallace Tower (Benholm's Lodging) in its original site at the junction of the Netherkirkgate and Carnegie's Brae. Although here captured at a time when it functioned as a hostelry, it was originally the 15th century fortified house of Sir Robert Keith of Benholm. The association with William Wallace is apocryphal.

Benholm's Lodging – now re-sited at Tillydrone, Seaton Park, is now Aberdeen's most historic council house – with apparently no takers.

The lower end of Union Street with Castle Street and Queen's Cross trams in operation. Walking on the street was possible, and indeed, was a necessity when alighting from or boarding trams.

A notable architectural 'plus' is the Royal Bank of Scotland (78-80 Union Street), erected in 1936, and, with its tall corinthian columns, argued to be the last classical bulding to be built in the street. The entrance to the contemporary Aberdeen Market is sharp right.

MARKET BUILDINGS, ABERDEEN. (BEFORE FIRE) 7052. G.W.W.

The interior of Aberdeen's New Market (1842) displaying its superb pitchpine roof and remarkable range of goods on sale. In 1882, forty years to the day after the building opened for business, a fire resulted in its total destruction. During the rebuilding period, many tenants opened up their own rival shops in other parts of the town.

The Aberdeen Market of the 1980's follows the traditions set by its predecessors by offering a range of goods from cassettes to candy.

UNION ST FACADE ABERDEEN, 535 . G.W.W.

AUL F1573

Cabs ply their trade in front of City Architect John Smith's striking granite frontage (1830) to St. Nicholas churchyard. The facade was conceived as a memorial to John Forbes of Newe, Strathdon.

With the exceptions of some additions to the roof spaces, only the street furniture, road markings and road surfaces have changed.

Aberdeen's 'Mither Kirk' is appropriately dedicated to St. Nicholas, patron saint of seamen, as befits a burgh with historic maritime traditions. Historically, the 'auld' (west) kirk catered for the Green and Crooked quarter, the 'new' (east) kirk for the Evin and Futty quarters.

WEST AND EAST PARISH CHURCHES, ABERDEEN.   10,290.   G.W.W.

St. Nicholas churchyard provides a resting place for many eminent Aberdonians, as well as a short cut from Schoolhill to Union Street.

AUL F4076

Brian Kiloh

Union Bridge, the Palace Hotel and the Northern Assurance Building in the days of electric trams. The Palace Hotel (left middle ground) displays the ambitions of the modestly named Great North of Scotland Railway Company, who developed it, for all to see. The north side of the bridge has already been widened (1905-8).

Fashions change and the bridge was widened again in 1964, with a set of buildings slapped on its southern side. The statue of Albert at the junction with Union Terrace is replaced by one of his son, Edward VII. The Prince Consort was demoted to the Schoolhill.

24

This view of Union Bridge postdates its widening in the early years of the 20th century when Kelly's Cats (William Kelly was the architect) were added to the new balustrade. The cats were inspired by the leopards on Aberdeen's heraldic burghal coat of arms.

Brian Kiloh

The Palace Hotel, once the jewel in the crown of the G.N.S. Railway Company is replaced by C and A's. The Commercial Union Assurance building with its Doric porch remains prominent in a view which still confirms the 1865 Imperial Gazetteer's assessment of Union Street as 'one of the finest streets in the Empire'.

Prince Albert presides over a gentle traffic flow governed by rails and overhead cables. As far as can be judged, pedestrian movements across the street are based on individual decision-making.

AUL F802

The contemporary view reveals traffic flow problems with 'no-go' boxes and filters. Pedestrian movements are by necessity more formalised.

Brian Kiloh

27

The original balustrade (and restricted width) of Union Bridge is evident in this late 19th century view. Patrons of the Palace Hotel (right foreground) could then enter the hotel direct by lift from the railway platform below.

In the contemporary view, fashions are more individualistic, and the pace of shopping increasingly frantic.

The Assembly Rooms (Music Hall) and residential middle Union Street in the days of the horse trams (which finally disappeared in Aberdeen in 1902). Union Bridge with its original constricted width and balustrade is visible in the distance.

Substantial modifications of the upper levels of buildings have taken place, and the original residential character of the street has been totally eroded by the world of commerce.

Union Street in the days of horse buses, highlighting (left foreground), the town residence of Sir Alexander Bannerman, the first house built on the street west of Union Bridge.

The clean uniform elevations of Victorian Union Street have been substantially modified, although the Assembly Rooms and Music Hall (1858) remain. Bannerman's residence, latterly the Royal Northern Club, was demolished in 1963.

Brian Kiloh

The narrowing vista towards Christ's College (1850 – originally the Free Church College) is framed by the Langstane and Gilcomston South churches. The originally residential character of Union Street, then populated by the professional classes, remains apparent.

The advantages of granite cassies when tramlines (or gas pipes) require attention are displayed in this contemporary view. The octagonal tower and dome of 208-210, Union Street (1911) is a notable plus to a vista which includes a number of architectural minuses.

The originally residential character of the buildings in Upper Union Street remains despite removal of railings and basement steps.

The relative narrowness of what was originally called Union Place (until 1890) has disappeared in this contemporary view, and shop awnings are no longer fashionable.

The Free Church College makes a fitting apex to the upper end of Union Street. The building in the right foreground was originally designed as a Waterhouse, its elegant frontage concealing a cistern which supplied much of early 19th century Aberdeen with its water supply. The same building was subsequently modified to house Aberdeen's best known horse bus enterprise.

FREE CHURCH COLLEGE, ABERDEEN. 10,932. G.W.W

The buildings remain in their essentials, but the basement entrances and railings have long since disappeared, and the groundfloor frontages are even more heavily modified (and frequently) as businesses come and go in the 1980's.

34

Boarding the Queen's Cross tram provided few problems for passengers in the absence of rival forms of mechanised transport.

Brian Kiloh

Although the double yellow peril is much in evidence, buses have the merit of picking up their customers from the relative safety of the pavements.

A pair of West End churches representing, in the background, Rubislaw Church (the Established Church – in sandstone – of 1875), and Queen's Cross Church (Free Church of 1881 – in granite). When this view was captured, Victoria's statue remained at the end of St. Nicholas Street.

The 'drooping lily' street lighting of 1989 contrasts with the elegant gas lighting of the Victorian view. The new buildings tacked onto Queen's Cross Church mark the growing involvement of churches in neighbourhood life throughout the week.

Queen's Cross (before the arrival of the statue) with the Rubislaw tram about to uplift passengers from the elaborate centre-piece of this five-road intersection. Picking up passengers from such positions must have been a feature unique to tramways.

Queen's Cross – Aberdeen's most terrifying rush-hour roundabout. The rather grand building at the corner of St. Swithin's Street was the residence of photographer George Washington Wilson.

Brian Kiloh

The gracious mansions and churches on Belmont Street, the former with well-tended gardens running down into the Den Burn valley, are juxtaposed with factories and slum property. Prince Albert (and friends) survey the scene.

Union Terrace before the statue of Prince Albert (1863) was shifted to Schoolhill (1914), and pre-dating the completion of His Majesty's Theatre. The Northern Assurance building (known to Aberdonians as 'the Monkey House') – a favourite rendezvous for socialisers – here featured without nighttime railings, forms a fitting corner to this elegant terrace.

AUL F4949

Edward VII replaces the Prince Consort in this prime corner site, with the arboreal descendants of the original Corby Heugh immediately behind, below which country lairds used to tether their horses before walking down to the Castlegate market.

Despite describing Aberdeen as 'a lazy town' during a brief visit in 1777, Robert Burns (here complete with daisy) merits a bronze statue on Union Terrace.

The valley of the lower Den Burn was for long a major barrier to Aberdeen's expansion to the west and north west. Houses on Belmont Street faced the open countryside until room for expansion was created by the construction of Union Bridge in 1805. The bridging of the valley by a viaduct in the 1880's is here clearly displayed.

The usage of the Den Burn floor as formal open space began in the 1780's with the erection of a public bath house, and regularisation of the channel. Although the burn disappeared underground in 1867 to make way for the Denburn Valley Railway, the construction of Union Terrace in the late 19th century, linking the viaduct with Union Street, provided a fitting backdrop for future floral displays.

The last couple of decades in the 20th century are bringing further change to the Schoolhill and Upperkirkgate with the Bredero development at last initiated.

George Jamieson's 16th century house ended its days as a lodging house before being demolished in the 1880's when the Schoolhill was straightened as part of the Rosemount Viaduct improvement package.

The granite pinnacles of Marischal College's North Wing and Mitchell Tower rise above the dense pack of buildings between St. Nicholas and George Streets. More people stand and converse on the streets than on the pavements.

Re-development between Broad Street and St. Nicholas Street successively for the new Municipal Buildings and the St. Nicholas Shopping Centre have practically effaced St. Nicholas Street, once the starting point of the turnpike to Inverurie. A further development scheme for lower George Street is ongoing.

The Marischal College frontage as completed in white Kemnay granite in 1906. The extensions owed much to the generosity of individual benefactors, notably Lord Strathcona and Charles Mitchell. Their heraldic shields are mounted above the entrance. This is the world's second largest granite building.

A gull's eye view of Marischal College and its fretwork profile.

The Marischal College Museum (mainly Anatomy and Natural History) with an exhibition featuring the anatomy of Man and the higher animals. Displaying the maximum of quantity was apparently the goal of the Victorian curator. A banquet of Victorian excess and monotony.

The much praised contemporary Anthropological Museum at Marischal College features displays which are thought-provoking and designed for all age groups.

Broad Street in the days of the College Gate Clothiery House, the Marischal College entrance archway and the Water House. Lord Byron lived in Broad Street lodgings when a boy.

Broad Street today is a product of 20th century architectural ideas – all cubes and pinnacles.

The Art Gallery (1882) and the
adjacent building designed for
Gray's School of Art, the latter
the product of the philanthropy of
engineer, John Gray, were built
on the site of the Old Grammar
School – hence Schoolhill.

Aberdeen's Art Gallery offers citizens and visitors
alike, an abiding treasure house of exhibitions,
including the Macdonald Collection of paintings,
donated in 1900, by the son of the granite
merchant who pioneered machine polishing of
Aberdeen's most famous export.

Aberdeen's Grammar School has been in existence for at least 550 years – a Town Grammar School existed in 1418. Its present building was completed in 1863, replacing its ancestor on the Schoolhill site. The building is here pictured without clock and statue of former pupil, Byron.

The Grammar School was seriously damaged by fire on 2 July, 1986. It continues to flourish despite the difficulties imposed by the need for use of temporary accommodation.

ART GALLERY, ABERDEEN. 14,891. G.W.W.

AUL.A2728

The Art Gallery, Schoolhill as it was before the War Memorial and Cowdray Hall were added at the western corner. The Gallery combines pink Corrennie with grey Kemnay granite.

53

The demands of traffic and roadworks intrude on the contemporary Schoolhill scene with pedestrians crossing with some difficulty.

The Sculpture Gallery extension of the Art Gallery was opened in 1905, and populated with classical Greco-Roman sculptures. The polished granite columns supporting the archways represent the best known British and Scandinavian products.

The contemporary displays of modern sculpture are set out in a friendlier and more casual atmosphere.

The inscriptions on the wall read:

MCMXIV   MCMXIX

TO
OUR
GLORIOUS
DEAD

MCMXXXIX   MCMXLV

The War Memorial (and Cowdray Hall) were tacked onto the end of the Art Gallery in 1925. The crescent-shaped colonnade (Kemnay granite) is fronted by a granite lion, sculptured by Aberdonian Arthur Taylor.

The Denburn Viaduct suburban
railway station (1893) is pictured
with a Great North of Scotland
Railway Company bus departing
for Newburgh. The little station
was latterly a tearoom before
being finally demolished in 1975.

The possibility of arriving by train from
Bucksburn (even, on occasion from
Peterculter) to patronise the threatre – in a
journey time of around 20 minutes – is alas,
no longer possible.

The statue of William Wallace (1888) displays from left to right, the three public buildings gracing the viaduct, namely Education, Salvation and Damnation (1891-1908) with muscle power remaining the principal form of wheeled propulsion. Note the small boys 'hinging on the back of the cart'.

Little change in the contemporary view save the demise of the granite cassies. St. Mark's Church apes the dome of St. Paul's in London, and was designed to be viewed from Union Bridge.

FREE SOUTH CHURCH & STATUE OF SIR WILLIAM WALLACE. 10,068. G.W.W.

St. Mark's Church with its striking dome, has a dignity which belies its parish kirk status. His Majesty's Theatre was yet to come in order to complete the viaduct trio of public buildings. The prominence given to the statue of Sir William Wallace despite the very considerable grants bestowed on Aberdeen by Robert the Bruce is a matter of some surprise to many Aberdonians.

Recent internal refurbishment of His Majesty's Theatre has created a superb asset for the city. Like St. Mark's, the Theatre sits on the very major engineering achievement of the Schoolhill-Rosemount Viaduct, which twice spans the deep valley of the Den Burn within a few hundred yards.

Brian Kiloh

60

The working faces, access tracks and derrick cranes of Rubislaw Quarry, of which it is said – with some truth – that much of Aberdeen came out of that hole.

RUBISLAW GRANITE QUARRIES, ABERDEEN

Scant respect is shown today to the hole that spawned most of Aberdeen's classier buildings.

A view from the Hill of Rubislaw looking down Queen's Road towards Rubislaw and Queen's Cross Churches. At that time, Rubislaw Quarry was virtually in the countryside.

The Duthie Park was gifted to the city in 1881 by Miss Elizabeth Crombie Duthie of Ruthrieston. Its ponds were fed by the waters of the Polmuir Burn. The park layout – originally designed for carriage drives – was formally opened to the public by Princess Beatrice in 1883.

The Gordon Memorial in the Duthie Park was erected by the Gordon Highlanders, Aberdeen City's own regiment, in memory of comrades who perished during the Egyptian Campaign.

The Duthie Park retains much charm even in winter, when, for the less hardy, floral abundance and even live music, are available in the heated Winter Gardens.

The Victoria Park (1871) – like Aberdeen's Duthie Park – belongs to an inner ring of Victorian parks, predating the city's boundary extensions of 1891.

The Victoria Park is notable in June for its rhododendrons and azaleas, and in July, for roses. Over 2 million roses have been planted in Aberdeen over the last 18 years. The park features a garden for the blind, with species recognisable by scent or touch.

Brian Kiloh

AUL E.2123

The Aberdeen Pierrots drew big audiences on the beach. Bathing huts are much in evidence. Mixed bathing on the beach and in the Bathing Station (1895) was not permitted until 1913.

Beach visitors in the 1980's tend to gravitate towards indoor entertainments.

The Queen's Links with, from left to right, the Bannermill, the Epidemic Hospital, and the Powder Magazine (on the skyline).

Open space still rules supreme on Aberdeen's Links.

The rock promontory of Girdleness acts as a great natural groyne trapping the beach sand which naturally moves alongshore in a southerly direction. Sand accumulations at the entrance to the Dee estuary necessitated the breakwater and pier construction in advance of major harbour works.

ON THE BEACH AT ABERDEEN. 2623. G.W.W.

AUL E1562

Brian Knox

Aberdeen's major tourist selling point in the 1960's was its designation as 'the silver city with the golden sands'. Its tourist profile in the 1980's has firmed up around floral displays and an enhanced range of city entertainments.

AUL F5498

AUL F4968

AUL F790

AUL F5462

Heavy seas sweep the new South Breakwater – a second attempt to protect the entrance to the port, made necessary by a sequence of extensions carried on to the North Pier.

Late Victorian urban surveying in the Shiprow (via navium) with Sopwith staff. Observe what happens to the window just above the surveyor's head in the following contemporary photograph.

The same house – Provost Ross's House of the 17th century – now restored and housing the Aberdeen Maritime Museum.

The Wellington Suspension Bridge (sometimes called the Chain Bridge) was built in 1830, partly with church funds, to provide access across the Dee for worshippers bound for Nigg Church. A toll was levied for pontage.

The new Queen Elizabeth bridge just downstream has been skilfully designed to remain physically subservient to the now pedestrianised Wellington Suspension Bridge.

Brian Kiloh

Guild Street with the Waverley Hotel and Her Majesty's Theatre (now the Tivoli) prominent, was built following reclamation of the intertidal flats of the Dee estuary.

A new office block occupies the site of the Caledonian Railway Station on Guild Street, with wheeled traffic clearly taking over from the rails.

AUL F4946

The electric tramway track to Torry recalls a period in Aberdeen's development when its citizens walked, cycled or took the tram to work. The relatively steep brae of Market Street (1840) was designed as a direct connection between harbour and city centre. Hotels then found major advantages in a central location.

Brian Kiloh

A proliferation of 'to let' signs indicate the increasing costs of a central location, while traffic flow, personalised in the earlier view, is now on a 'first come, first served' basis.

The smoky city with chimneys, tall and short, dominating the view towards the Victoria Dock.

AUL F801

ABERDEEN HARBOUR FROM THE MUNICIPAL TOWER . 2638 .G.W.W.

A view from the New Town House across Marischal Street towards the Victoria Dock in the days when sail was queen.

A general view of Aberdeen Harbour, now entirely tidal, and geared up for North Sea oil and gas business.

ABERDEEN HARBOUR . 2890. C.W.W.

Fishing boats, squareriggers and steamers mingle in Aberdeen's Outer Harbour. The Sheerlegs sited just outside the dock-gates were designed for installing engines in vessels, at a time when Aberdeen boasted three shipyards.

The Victoria Dock from just inside the dock-gates with barques moored along Blaikie's Quay. When Queen Victoria landed in Aberdeen in 1848, this dock, although not then entirely completed, was regarded as one of the wonders of the British Empire.

A contemporary view from Pocra displays Hall Russells, the last of the shipbuilding companies in Aberdeen, the cranes of Matthew's Quay and the now entirely tidal nature of the port.

Unloading and bagging coal in Aberdeen's Upper Dock, prior to distribution throughout the city by horse and cart. The high clock tower of the Harbour Offices (1885) was designed to be seen throughout the docks.

Cranes break the skyline instead of brick chimneys. The dominance of road traffic is reflected in the Ro-Ro facility on the left and the Northern Isles vehicular access ramp on the right.

Brian Kiloh

ABERDEEN. FROM TORRY. 1249. G.W.W.

AUL E2258

Herring boats were drawn up along the southern banks of the newly diverted Dee. The infant Albert Basin is still under development, the surrounding reclaimed land largely unoccupied. The skyline is broken by the New Town House, the Old Tolbooth, the North Church and the Castlehill Barracks.

The ground remains well tended, but the opening of the Victoria Bridge in 1881 opened up the lands of Torry to residential development, much of it originally connected with the fishing industry and its profits.

ABERDEEN FROM BALNAGASK.   10,073.   G.W.W.

The Dee has been successfully diverted into its entirely artificial channel, permitting the reclamation of land for herring landings and curing stations. In the 1878 season (May-August), 93,000 barrels were filled with herring for export to the Baltic countries.

85

Oil supply bases replace parts of Lower Torry, and sediment and fuel tanks occupy the former curing stances on **Mearns** and **Albert Quays**. High rise blocks dominate the skyline as the city spreads upwards and outwards.

Brian Kiloh

AUL E1563

The fleet leaves harbour in late afternoon or early evening. Signs of steam, which was to revolutionise the industry towards the end of the 19th century are visible on the horizon.

A group of Inverness-registered 'stranger boats' are manoeuvring with sail and oars to enter harbour under light winds. The highly perishable nature of the product often caught up to 50 miles offshore explains the desire to reach harbour as quickly as possible.

AUL E108

AUL E109

A group of Aberdeen-registered boats, again under favourable winds, struggle to reach port. Paddle tugs were often employed to tow groups of boats into the curing stations.

Loads of fish were landed in the Old Fish Market in the days of steam.

AUL F3743

Aberdeen remains the prime fish processing centre in North Britain although gathering its raw material from a variety of landing points. The new Fish Market displays a confidence in the future of the industry.

King's College frontage with manse and Old Brewery chimney – a formidable combination of Elphinstone's early 16th century chapel and Crown Tower and John Smith's Gothic west front (1832). The Crown Tower was built by the same mason who worked on St. Giles in Edinburgh.

Brian Kiloh

The removal of the railings and pillars evokes a more relaxed atmosphere to university life in the 1980's, with New King's (1912) and Elphinstone's Memorial (1911) making their appearance as elements in a 20th century quadrangle alongside the original one.

A rear view of King's College featuring the ivy-clad Round Tower with its low angle conical roof. The 16th century tower dates from a time when the infant Catholic university found the need to defend itself against the excesses of the Reformation.

The Sports Pavilion (1939-41) was considered extremely avant garde and modernist for its period, but offers fine views across the playing field. The Round Tower (complete with shot loops) lurks behind the Pavilion.

Where in Earth?

The west front of St. Machar Cathedral consists of martial granite towers surmounted by sandstone spires. Its great central tower collapsed in the 17th century.

The austere exterior of St. Machar Cathedral conceals a superb heraldic ceiling, reflecting the Christian unity of Europe prior to the events of the Reformation.

The Bridge of Don was opened in 1830 as a much needed improvement on the picturesque but narrow Brig of Balgownie.

The bridge was widened and strengthened in 1958, while retaining architect John Smith's masonry.

The Brig of Balgownie across the gorge of the Don, although established as a single-arched bridge in the 14th century, was largely rebuilt in the 17th century, when it remained the main route north from the town.

AUL C8135

Brian Kiloh

A fund of money for the upkeep of the bridge established at the time of the early 17th century reconstruction in time accumulated sufficient revenue to pay for the early 19th century replacement Bridge of Don (1830).

The Sparkling Cage

by John S. Smith

Brian Kiloh in the footsteps of
George Washington Wilson

 **AUL**

Published by Keith Murray Publications,
46 Portal Crescent, Tillydrone, Aberdeen, Scotland. AB2 2SP
and
Aberdeen University Library, Queen Mother Library, Meston Walk, Aberdeen AB9 2UE
First published 1989
Printed and Typeset by Halcon Printing Ltd., Stonehaven.

ISBN 1 870978 13 7

Acknowledgements

Mike Craig and Caroline Gilbert of the Aberdeen University photographic department for their skills in producing first class prints from the GWW source.
John Smith Jnr. for his assistance in helping us map a sequential route throughout the book.
Alan Young for his contribution of several modern photographs.
Iain Crichton Smith for permission to use his poem 'Aberdeen' from his selected poems, Carcanet Press.
A special thank you to Mary Murray of the Special Collections Department of Aberdeen University for her co-operation and encouragement.

Cover Designed by Innes Taylor, 1989.

Prints of the modern photographs may be purchased from Keith Murray Publications.
Prints of the early photographs may be purchased from Aberdeen University Library.
The source of each photograph is credited alongside it.

Abbreviations

AUL   Aberdeen University Library, George Washington Wilson Collection.
ACL   Aberdeen City Library, Local Studies Collection.